Northampton In Camera

by
Rosemary Babbington

QUOTES LIMITED

MCMXCIV

Published by Quotes Limited
Whittlebury, England

Typeset in Plantin by
Key Composition, Northampton, England

Pictures Lithographed by
South Midlands Lithoplates Limited, Luton, England

Printed by Busiprint Limited
Buckingham, England

Bound by WBC Bookbinders Limited
Bridgend, Glamorgan

© Rosemary Babbington 1994

ISBN 0 86023 621 8

Acknowledgements

In 1970, I met Peter Golding who was taking photographs of all the buildings which were being pulled down in the town. We made this into a booklet and all profits went to the Northampton and County Association for the Blind. My children, Cathy and Rob tell me that now is a good time to bring out this new book as, of course, the new buildings have been completed.

In that first book *Momento, a century of change in Northampton*, I thanked many people who helped make that work possible — they will forgive me if I do not repeat them all by name. I remain grateful to them, and hope that this new book, containing some of their material, advice and encouragement, will bring its own reward.

With the new book I am further indebted to the County Council's Education and Libraries Department, and especially David Dean and Marion Arnold, for the loan of postcards and photographs. Similarly, Alan Burman, the *Chronicle and Echo*, Mrs W. Craddock, Boots the Chemists, Northampton & District Hospital Management Committee, British Rail, Peter Golding and the *Northampton Independent* supplied pictures used in both publications. I have also to thank Mr R. Warwick.

Local historian Clive Birch located, acquired and lent numerous further pictures to complete this book and helped with the text and Toni MacReady took the modern photographs to complete the book.

Key to Caption Credits

AB	Alan Burman	PG	P. Golding
CB	Clive Birch	NI	*Northampton Independent*
BC	Boots the Chemists	CC	Northants Libraries
BR	British Rail	NH	Northampton Hospital
CE	*Chroncile & Echo*	TMN	Tony MacReady
WC	Mrs W. Craddock		

3

In the 1970s Northampton entered a phase of development and change. It was then that the idea was born for *Momento, a Century of Change* — an inexpensive booklet supported by a local grant, and by advertisements from sympathetic local firms. That private publication earnt much-needed funds for the Northampton & District Association for the Blind. It also set out to record the rapidly changing townscape.

I cannot do better than repeat some of what Colin Robinson wrote then in his generous foreword: 'That Northampton pictured in these pages is fast disappearing before our eyes. Almost half of our town centre area, as well as great chunks beyond, has been or is being demolished, re-shaped and re-built in a series of frantic convulsive upheavals of more than blitz-like proportions. The scale of these operations is possibly unequalled in any other town or city of comparable size.

'Surely there is grim irony in all this? When it seemed that one way of limiting London's teeming millions was to disperse a proportion of the population into the provinces, Northampton was chosen as one recipient of this massive transplant operation because, amongst other reasons, it has an historic and well-defined established character of its own.

'This, it was claimed, would help newcomers soon feel at home and assimilate into an already existing community. There was undoubted logic in its thinking. That feeling of being uprooted could be less devastating than starting life afresh in a completely new town.

'What was obviously not realised was that, under the impact of this population influx, much of that established character would be bulldozed out of existence.' Mr Robinson went on to ask if the emerging town centre was likely to be very much different from any other 'new town' or the areas our newcomers had left. Perhaps those of us who were here before, and remain still, can answer that; certainly, the newcomers may be surprised at what they missed, what has disappeared.

Colin Robinson wrote about good buildings of the past — not the fine ones that have survived, but the ordinary yet 'bright gems' lining originally medieval streets and Market Square. He saw that those very buildings, neither grand or continuous, might be lost in the drive to modernise. To some extent he was right.

We would all agree that the way of life reflected by 'factories, warehouses, shops, market, pubs, places of entertainment and worship, streets of terraced houses, fine town houses, all packed together' has radically changed, and ours is much more a town for commuters, side street businesses in one-time homes, superstore and precinct, corporate structure and car park complex, not to mention the ubiquitous car and its corresponding, greedy partner, the road.

In these pages you will find some of those 'bright gems' of the past, some that have somehow survived, scenes that have changed but still contain something of our heritage and some vistas that you will be hard-placed to recognise at all. It will also serve to remind us that no living townscape remains still; there will always be change, some good, some bad. Whatever the changes, Northampton is still a good place to be and I hope this album of its past appeals to both native and newcomer and helps us treasure what remains of that past, while striving to produce tomorrow's 'bright gems'.

This is a photo of a painting of a woodcut — originally Edward Pretty drew the cattle market of c1847, then local artist J. A. Perrin painted this scene, photographed for the record in our own day. The cattle, sheep and pig market was held on Saturdays. (CC)

LEFT: Market Square in 1870 was still used for cattle, but three years later, a new custom-built market was opened off Victorian Promenade. The fountain went up in 1863 and came down in 1962. It commemorated the marriage of the future Edward VIII. Its plinth resisted removal until 1972. (CC) RIGHT: All Saints' Parish Church was the destination of this 1900s two-horsed, garden-seat omnibus. (CB)

Kingsthorpe Mill has long gone; in 1864 C. FitzHugh was the miller. Here it is some thirty years later. (CC)

Kingsthorpe High Street has survived; in this picture of the 1900s, it was traffic-free and gaslit. (CC)

This horse trams, sometimes called a horse car, was at the junction of St Leonard's and Haines Roads, Far Cotton in the 1890s. The service lasted for around twenty years. Christy's Tea was sold in the shop on the left and advertised on the 'bus. (AB)

In the 1900s, horsed trams served Mercer's Row, here passing the London City and Midland Bank; the driver is now downstairs, the trams are running on rails, and the stairs at the front suggest one-man operation is not that new a practice. (CC)

By the 1900s the Market Square had developed a plethora of stalls, Sarsaparilla and Lime Juice Beverage is the flavour of the day in the foreground at one old penny a glass, and the clock stands at twenty past seven. Gaslighting is evident and the background buildings include the Northampton Mercury, Harry Jones, spectacle-maker and bootmaker Hunt — a typical cross-section in the heart of the town. (CB)

By contrast to the bustling scene overleaf, the Edwardian Market Square shows us empty space, sophisticated open and covered transport — a growler, a cab and a small landau and a curious throng around what appears to be a small sideshow, perhaps a Punch and Judy, in front of the fountain, with at least one official in tricorn hat in attendance. Behind are the Peacock Commercial and Midland Railway Hotel, demolished in 1960, the Post Horn pub, the Lord Palmerston Hotel, the Northampton Herald, the Three Tuns Inn and, on the right, the 'Modern Ready Money Drapery Establishment' of Cole and Hughes. (CC)

The electric tram service started in 1904 — here are two on their inaugural run, passing the main entrance of Abington Park. (CC)

The tramlines posed a hazard in Abington Street, where horsed transport still reigned supreme; the Bantam Cock inn was on the left and Ruggers, opticians, on the right, c1905. The Central Library replaced these shops five years later.
(CB)

The Tramcar Tavern on the left in St James' End was demolished some twenty years ago. It was a popular fare stage for the service which gave it name and custom, bound here for Kingsley Park. (CC)

The dominant building in 1901 was the new Emporium Arcade in Market Square, which offered a restaurant, gym, hairdressing, 50 shops, a café and public toilets. It was lit by electricity. The Arcade was demolished in 1972. Among the traders of that year were Whiting's piano and organ showrooms and Harry Jones' spectacles shop. (CC)

One 1904 destination for travellers by tram was Kingsthorpe — this is Harborough Road, with Thornton Park in the background, and the Cock tavern on the left of the impressive range of buildings to the right. (CC)

Abington Church and the Abbey in Abington Park — from an early postcard published by R. Harris & Son of 6 Bridge Street; there was a small convent in Abington Street in the 1860s. (CB)

18

Abington Street with the New Theatre on the left and the Notre Dame High School on the right, previously the Convent, and demolished c1975. (CC)

The New Theatre was opened in 1912. It lasted forty six years, coming down in 1960. In its first year it presented Florence Esdale, Roma and Romani, Almasio and Yamina and Harry Drew. In its final years it attracted household names like Gracie Fields, but it could not compete with television. To see Frank Elliston & Co in 'Three and a Fool' you paid nine old pennies for a place in the orchestra pit. (WC)

The Market Square as it looked some seventy years ago — virtually all these buildings have disappeared: the shops on the corner of Newland, the fountain, the lamp posts, the Arcade, and a majority of the other buildings up to the skyline. The sheer variety of commerce is staggering, from Higgins the drapers to the Peacock Hotel, from Abel & Sons the music people to the Liverpool, London and Globe Insurance Co, and from Haylock's boots to the Mercury newspaper. (CC)

All Saints' Church was one of four parish churches in the 1860s archdeaconry of Northampton. Rebuilt after the devastating town fire of 1675, it retained its original square tower with a new cupola on top. Here it is seen from St Giles' Square in the late 1920s. George Row on the left was named after the George Hotel, which stood at the top of Bridge Street. The Cenotaph is in the foreground. (CB)

Bridge Street ushers in the motorcar era, and the beginnings of change in the townscape, the Bell Hotel on the right. (CC)

The North Western Hotel dominates the left hand side of Gold Street in the horse tram days of early this century. (CC)

Electric power brought larger capacity trams in 1904 — here in the bustling Gold Street with gaslighting and narrow pavements. (CC)

In 1913 the top of Gold Street looked like this. You could buy your watch at H. Samuel and insure it with Atlas Assurance upstairs. Cars were appearing, horses were prevalent and the trams carried those who did not twist their ankles negotiating both cobbled streets and tramlines. (CC)

Guildhall on the left and County Hall on the right in 1917. The latter was built in the Italian style as a courthouse and the centre of administration for the county. (CC)

LEFT: Guildhall, here in the 1930s, was built in St Giles Square in 1864 and extended in 1982. (CB) RIGHT: The splendid Cromwell House in Marefair, which is now called Hazelrigg House. It is Elizabethan and allegedly Cromwell stayed here before the Battle of Naseby. (CB)

Coker & Co were general leather merchants in Abington Square, where Charles Bradlaugh's statue directed the traffic. He was an honest MP for Northampton, an atheist who helped the poor, and died in 1899. (CB)

St Giles was one of three parish churches in the 19th century — its tower is reputedly 17th century and the original 12th century church was extensively restored in the mid-19th century. (CC)

St Edmund's was carved out of St Giles' Parish in the 1860s; the building was consecrated in 1852, and has been pulled down. (CC)

St Peter's is the third of the original four nineteenth century parishes. It is near the site of the Norman castle, and claims Norman origins; it was restored in the 1860s. (CC)

LEFT: The fourth parish was that of the Holy Sepulchre, or St Sepulchre's, an unusual round edifice traced to the Knight's Templar, and given his inimitable treatment by Sir Giles Gilbert Scot t in the 1860s. (CC) RIGHT: Queen Eleanor's Cross, London Road, one of the enduring landmarks of the town, erected in 1290 to mark a stage in the Queen's funeral procession from Nottinghamshire to Westminster. (CB)

OPPOSITE LEFT: Of many other churches and chapels, the College Street Baptist Chapel was replaced by this handsome building in the 1860s. (CB) RIGHT: St Mary's Church, Towcester Road, Far Cotton, was built in 1885 — an attractive design. Due to the new roundabout at St Leonards traffic can now leave Far Cotton without using Bridge Street. (CB) ABOVE LEFT: Houses in a court off Bridge Street, drawn by J. Standley Adams in the early twenties; RIGHT: Adams' view of Silver Street, partly demolished for the fish market.

36

OPPOSITE: Locock's Hill, Sheep Street, drawn by Standley Adams in the 1920s. ABOVE: The General Hospital and King Edward Memorial. (CB)

OPPOSITE: The Hospital in Billing Road before extensions were built in the 1930s. The roads leading off left and right were York, Alexandra and Denmark Roads. (NH) ABOVE: Nurses pause between chores in this 1920s picture in Northampton Hospital laundry. (NH)

Mercer's Row, with the Westminster Bank and Boots, a Co-op van passing All Saints' Church on the right. (CB)

In the centre of the town, it is easy to forget that it is built on the northern slopes above the river Nen, Nyne or, as we call it, Nene. In 1905 South Bridge looked like this. (CB)

The Lock and river Nene in 1918. (CB)

Mayorhold in the 1930s — a busy 'bus terminus, it was demolished for the dual carriageway from Regent Square to St Peter's Way. (CE)

Northampton School for Girls in St George's Avenue in 1934. The building has survived, but the school is now in Spinney Hill Road. (CB)

Abington Street was widened in the 1940s, the old telephone exchange coming down in the process. (CE)

London and North Western Railway's Castle Station — the line was in 1864 'a branch railway from Blisworth station . . . touching this town on its way to Peterborough: by these means a facility of communication is obtained with almost every part of the kingdom, which has added much to the prosperity of the town ' — renovated in 1963.
(CB)

Bridge Street Station, in 1948; this was the first railhead in the town, opened in 1847 and now gone. (BR)

Ireson House, Bath Street was a large and attractive stone house demolished in the central area development scheme which affected the area around the Mayorhold. This 'Spanish' backyard was an ink factory, drawn by T. Osborne Robinson OBE before demolition.

The Northampton Co-operative Society and the public library dominated the streetscene in the 1950s, when half cab motor 'buses had become the norm for public transport. (CB)

The last private house in Abington Street was demolished for shops in the 1950s. (CE)

LEFT: *Rheinfilden, drawn by T. Osborne Robinson OBE, before its demolition in 1961; it was built in 1876 and demolished in 1961. RIGHT: The Market Square in the 1960s — the second largest in the land. (PG)*

St Peter's Way was in the planning stages when this shot was taken in June 1958. (NI)

Another picture in the same 1958 series has the arrows to show where St Peter's Way would go. (NI)

Redevelopment has altered the five acres between Market Square and the Mounts beyond recognition. Here are Abel's and the Emporium Arcade on Market Square — demolished.

54

Kerr Street was one of the streets that lost out to development; the police station on the Mounts is in the background.
(PG)

LEFT: *The Emporium Arcade in the original architect's drawing of 1901; Moseley & Scrivener designed it and it was built on the site of the orchard and garden of Parade House by A. Chown. Sixteen billiard tables enhanced its inter-war reputation. It once had 150 shops. Now gone, its archway has been stored for safekeeping. RIGHT: Temperance Hall, built 1886, became one of the longest-running cinemas in the country. (PG)*

LEFT: Masonic Hall, Princess Street was erected in 1890. RIGHT: Lady's Lane, named after a then nearby statue of Our Lady of Grace. (PG)

Black Lion Hill, opposite Castle Station, before road widening, with Mannings Brewery. (PG)

Leading into Gold Street was Mare Fair, between Gold Street and Black Lion Hill — demolished in the 1960s.
(CB)

LEFT: The Quart Pot, later a shop and RIGHT: the North Western Hotel, both gone. (PG)

St Andrew's Church and the surrounding area made way for the then new dual carriageway in the seventies, along with Broad Street and part of Regent Square. (PG)

LEFT: Broad Street looking towards Regent Square and RIGHT: the demolished Albion Club. (PG)

LEFT: Broad Street looking towards Mayorhold and RIGHT: a house which once graced Regent Square. (PG)

Lost pubs — LEFT: the Ram Hotel, Sheep Street lost out to a multi-storey car park; RIGHT: the King's Head and Green Dragon, Mayorhold — gone. (PG)

An office block went up on this site opposite St Sepulchre's. (PG)

LEFT: This bridge in Bridge Street has gone; RIGHT: so have these buildings in St James' Square. (PG)

ABOVE: These shops in Abington Street, at the corner of Wood Street, went to make way for redevelopment. (CE)
BELOW: Northampton Bus Station in Derngate in 1936. (CC)

Threatened by the expressway in the 1970s, these streetscenes are now no more: Barrack Road/Regent Square.

Clare Street School.

Billing Road/Cliftonville.

Regent Square, east side.

Spencer Bridge Road.

Drill Hall, Clare Street.

Some scenes stay the same, like this early view of Thomas à Becket's Well near Victorian Promenade; it was so called because the Archbishop drank its waters, and the well never dried up after his murder. (CB)

New buildings may one day be tomorrow's threatened species — will we care so much about them? Here are the Law Courts. (TM)

The extension to the Guildhall is one of the future's 'bright gems'. (TM)

Office block on Marefair. (TM)

The Grosvenor Centre. (TM)

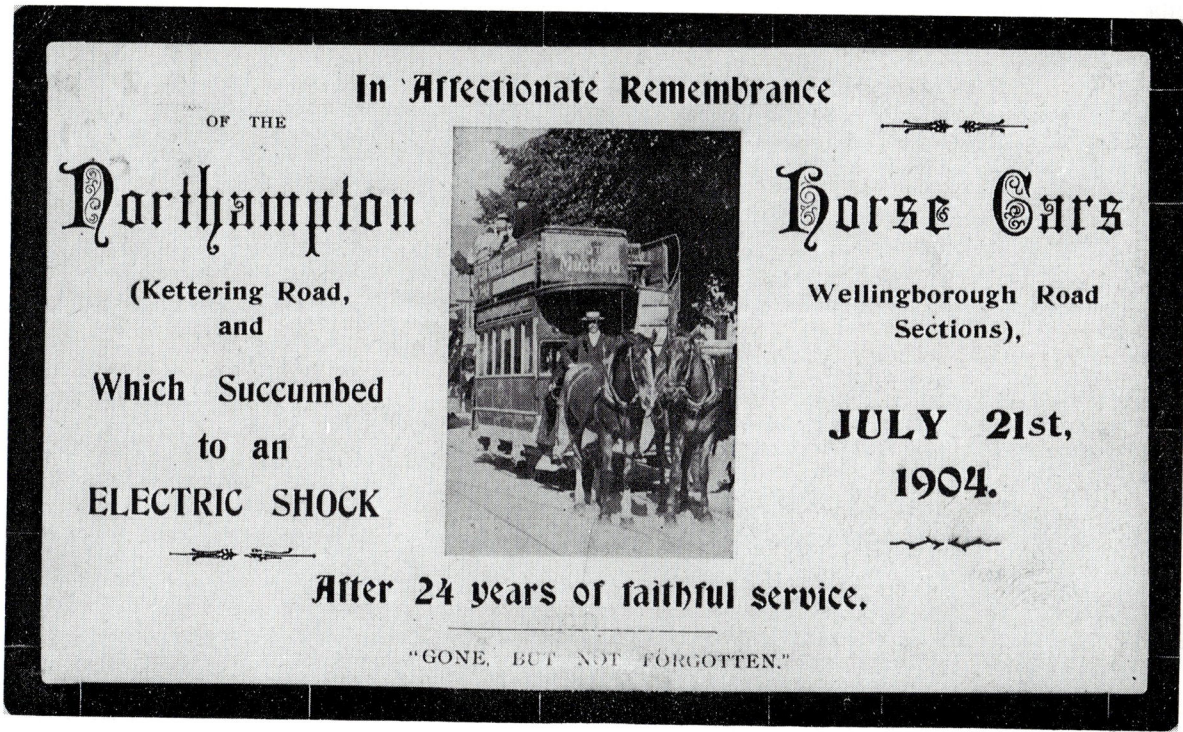

In Affectionate Remembrance

OF THE

Northampton

(Kettering Road, and

Which Succumbed

to an

ELECTRIC SHOCK

Horse Cars

Wellingborough Road Sections),

JULY 21st, 1904.

After 24 years of faithful service.

"GONE, BUT NOT FORGOTTEN."

This card, posted 21 July 1904, records the passing of the horse tramcars, and perhaps reflects the same sentiments towards the vanished buildings of Northampton in these pages — 'Gone but not forgotten'.

Index to Illustrations